Signature

of a

LEADER

Follow the steps

to

INSPIRED LEADERSHIP

By

GRANT NORLIN

Special Thanks To

Val Norlin – For being my sounding board, editor and wife.

Nicole Matthews – For editing, cover design and being my daughter.

AND

To the great people of the
CALGARY FOOTHILLS BRANCH

CONTENTS

PROLOGUE

After 30 years of leading an organization comprised of sales people, salaried staff and entrepreneurs... I retired.

My office held a retirement party in my honour and presented me with a photo album depicting pictures of people and events that spanned my thirty year career.

In addition to the photos, I found numerous cards and letters from my associates that were very flattering to read. They wrote about the effect of my leadership on their lives and careers.

No one wrote about my weaknesses. While reading their kind comments I thought about what happens at a person's funeral. Tributes given at a time like that make the person sound like a saint. I knew I wasn't one.

As I re-read the tributes sometime later, I realized these people were writing about things I had done that were important to **them**, not mistakes that I might have made.

A few weeks later I received an email from one of my former associates who was taking a course on leadership and they were using **me** as an example. They sent me the material they had written and I was, quite frankly, *blown away*. I said to my wife, "You have to read this! I can't believe the things they are saying."

My wife read it and asked why I was surprised. She said, "That's you. That's who you are." That is the first time I realized that I was an *'UNCONSCIOUS COMPETENT'*

People tend to fall into four categories:

1. **CONSCIOUS COMPETENT**: This person is good at what they do and knows why. He/she is the type of person that can describe, in detail, what they do that has made them successful. They can write books about it, hold training seminars describing their techniques, etc.

2. **UNCONSCIOUS COMPETENT**: This person is good at what they do, but feels what they do is only natural. Just common sense. He/she thinks everyone understands it. Describing successful techniques in detail is very difficult because this person does things as a matter of course. No big deal.

3. **CONSCIOUS INCOMPETENT**: This person is aware that they are not that good at some things and are fully aware of their weaknesses.

4. **UNCONSIOUS INCOMPETENT**: This person is not good at some things and is most likely unaware that he/she is not good. If they are aware, they don't know what they are doing wrong.

These four traits can be found in all kinds of people: Athletes, parents, politicians, writers or business executives.

To help you understand the difference, look at the careers of two famous golfers, Tom Kite and Ben Crenshaw. They are both Texan's and their careers followed similar paths. Their winning record was almost identical and both were coached by Harvey Penick in their younger years.

Tom was a **CONSCIOUS COMPETENT**. He liked to understand the mechanics of a golf swing etc. and when Harvey taught him, he focused on those details. Tom would be able to describe all aspects of his game and explain them in detail.

Ben was an **UNCONSCIOUS COMPETENT**. In other words, he was a NATURAL. He would be called a *FEEL* player.

Harvey writes about his first meeting with Ben, who was a very good, very young golfer. Harvey put a ball on the tee on a par three and told Ben to hit it onto the green. Ben did. They walked to the green and Harvey told Ben to putt it into the hole. Ben's answer was, "Why didn't you tell me on the tee box that you wanted it in the hole?"

He was seven years old at the time and didn't see any reason why he couldn't have put the ball in the hole right from the tee! He wasn't focused on *HOW* he would have done it, like a conscious competent would have been.

After retiring, I discovered that when it came to leadership skills, I was an **UNCONSCIOUS COMPETENT** and that is why some of the things said about me came as a complete surprise.

The second thing I learned happened later on.

I decided to read all of the notes and cards again, but not from an ego standpoint. I wanted to learn what specific things about my leadership were important to these people who had taken the time to write this stuff down.

When I looked at the list that I compiled I was very surprised. They did not write about complicated psychological thoughts or ideas. Rather, what they wrote was so simple, that anyone could learn and put these ideas into practise. There is no advanced training required, and these skills can be used by people in all walks of life. They apply to business, sports, and even dealing with family members.

THE RISK to you as you read these **Lessons in Leadership** will be to minimize some of the ideas because they seem too simple.

PLEASE DON'T.

EXCELLENCE IN LEADERSHIP is not complicated, once you understand it.

RESERVED FOR YOUR THOUGHTS

LESSON ONE
JUST SAY THANKS

A leader should always remember that the people associated with them are there because they CHOSE to be there.

Now, you might be saying that you *HIRED* them to your company, or *RECRUITED* them to your football team, or *INVITED* them to join your choir. That may be true, but they said YES. They could have joined a different company, or team, or choir.

How do I know that? If you are a great leader you only invite top people to join you. You did not look for the easiest hire, or pick from the bottom of the list, you went after the **best**. If they are the **best**, other leaders would welcome them with open arms.

They are with you because **they chose you**.

You should always be thankful for their decision and let them know on a regular basis that you appreciate them.

Some leaders have the attitude of ENTITLEMENT. They are the boss. They EXPECT the best from their people. They are running a business, or a team, or a choir and are not there to babysit their associates. The reward their associates should expect is their pay, or adulation from the fans or audience. A Christmas bonus is nice, a card on their birthday is appreciated, but there is something more appreciated, and easier to deliver, and that is... to say:

"THANKS!"

RESERVED FOR YOUR THOUGHTS

"GREAT JOB!"

"I REALLY APPRECIATE YOU!"

Easy to do, cost's you nothing, gets great mileage and is RARELY USED by some leaders.

Why is that? I'm not sure, but I learned from the material given to me on my retirement that **people want to feel APPRECIATED, more than any other reward.**

As we leaders go through our busy day we should remember that:

THE PEOPLE ASSOCIATED WITH YOU ARE THERE BECAUSE THEY CHOOSE TO BE, AND THEY WANT TO FEEL APPRECIATED.

Just say THANKS.

It is *SO EASY* and *SO VERY IMPORTANT.*

LESSON TWO
PEOPLE WITH LIVES

The people associated with you are REAL PEOPLE with families, hopes and dreams, worries, concerns. They are not just EMPLOYEES, ATHLETES OR CHOIR MEMBERS.

When I walked into my office, the first person I saw was the receptionist. I often stopped for a moment to ask how her weekend went. If I knew her child was ill, or involved in something important to them, I would ask about it.

Sometimes when talking with one of our people I would share some small detail about my golf game or something about my personal life.

No big deal. I never gave it much thought, until I read some of the letters after my retirement.

I discovered that not only did they want to be regarded as PEOPLE WITH LIVES, but they wanted to know about ME as a PERSON WITH A LIFE and not just their leader.

When it comes right down to it, we are all the same in many ways. We just have different titles and responsibilities.

Years ago, my wife and I went to Hilton Head, South Carolina. In the mornings we would see buses filled with mostly African American people come onto the island. They would cut the grass; clean the rooms, serve meals, and then leave on the bus at the

RESERVED FOR YOUR THOUGHTS

end of the day. We didn't know them, or know anything about them. They were employees of the resort *just doing their job.*

We decided to go to a church where we were the only white people in attendance. When we arrived we saw some of the "workers" we had seen earlier. They were all dressed up. Some of the dresses their little girls wore were bright and colorful. Their hair was done up with bows and they sang as they entered the church. Families sat together, laughed together................

They were regular people, just like us. They had families, dreams and hopes for their future.

They were just like us, they just had a different "title".

The people you work with want you to remember that they are **PEOPLE WITH LIVES, AND NOT JUST EMPLOYEES.**

It's *SO EASY* to do; cost's you nothing and is *SO IMPORTANT.*

RESERVED FOR YOUR THOUGHTS

LESSON THREE
REALLY LISTEN

People want you to LISTEN to them... REALLY LISTEN.

I went to a management meeting a few years ago where the speaker talked about how he ran his business, and he talked about listening.

He told us that early each day he would walk down the hall, poke his head into each office he came to and say "Hi, How are things,", or something like that. Before that person could give him a full answer he was already at the next office.

One of his people got tired of that routine. The next day when the manager poked his head into his office and asked his routine question, that man said "My mother died last night". The manger quickly said "great" and headed for the next door.

When the employee later mentioned this to the manager, he was shocked. The manager thought he was being friendly and doing a good thing with his daily tour.

That manger would have been better off, if he only took time to talk with a few people each day, and **really LISTEN**, then to try to whiz through the whole office and actually accomplish nothing.

Many of the letters I received dealt with this topic. Statements like "when I talked to you I felt I had your full attention".

My office was at the corner of the building. I could see people

coming and going. The natural thing to do when someone passed by my door and waved was to wave back. If you have someone in your office at that time and you wave to a person walking by, for that brief moment, the person in your office does not have your full attention. They feel it. We have all been in the position at some type of gathering, when we are talking to someone and their eyes are glancing around the room to see who is there. It feels as though we are talking to ourselves and the person we are speaking with is definitely not really interested in what we are saying. Not a very rewarding conversation.

When someone was talking with me in my office, my phone was put on pause, I often shut the door, and I definitely paid no attention to people walking down the hall.

I never thought much about that. It just seemed like the right thing to do. The letters I received clarified that for me.

When you are talking with a person, be **WITH THAT PERSON**, and let them feel they are the most important person to you at that moment.

It is SO EASY to do and SO IMPORTANT.

RESERVED FOR YOUR THOUGHTS

LESSON FOUR
TRAINING

When it comes right down to it, you need leaders, but the people you lead are the ones who make or break it for you. The ideas may stem from management but they are performed by others.

There are some basics of training:

1. Your employees must know very clearly what their job is. An outsider should be able to ask an employee what their job is and a clear and concise answer should be on the tip of their tongue.

2. They must know how to do it. They need to master every aspect of their job and be able to perform it on "auto pilot".

3. They must have all of the tools they need to perform it and those tools must work without a hitch.

4. They need to know what you expect the final outcome to be, and to know that you will inspect from time to time.

5. Then you have to leave them alone and let them do their job.

If a manager performs the first four points but not the fifth, that manager becomes a micro manager, slows progress and reduces the employee's confidence.

RESERVED FOR YOUR THOUGHTS

The challenge for management is to make sure points 1-4 get done. We might be surprised how many people cannot give a clear answer to point one.

Try it sometime. Ask the person working in the back shop at your golf course, or the music director at your church, or the receptionist at your doctor's office.

Point # 5 is the most difficult for many leaders. It is difficult to give responsibility for a good result to someone else when in the back of your mind you know, or think, you can do it better.

I was a manager of a life insurance organization which is very much performance driven. Sales results are very measurable and as a manager I always wanted to see the month end results. On one occasion I knew the month had been fantastic and was so excited to see the results that I went into my office at night as I knew the results would be coming in, on the computer.

My office manager would take the results each month and prepare a bulletin that would show the performance in many categories. That night I decided to help her out. I took the data off the computer, did all of the calculations that she would need to prepare the bulletin, and then went home quite proud of myself. I *knew* I had done my office manager a great favor.

The next morning I handed her the sheets showing the work I had done. She looked at me, then at the pages, then back at me again. She then took the pages, threw them in the garbage, and said,

"Thanks but we have our own way of doing it." Ouch.................

I failed point # 5.

The good news, however, is she felt she had the right to do what she did, and her job was not on the line.

I felt better when I thought about that.

All five points in the training program are essential to obtain top results.

They are *NOT* easy to do but *EXTREMELY* important.

RESERVED FOR YOUR THOUGHTS

LESSON FIVE
WHO DOES THE LEADER TALK TO?

This can be a tough one. During my career I always had a management team. We shared thoughts and ideas freely. Nothing held back. Our meetings were 'safe' places to express ourselves but, this team was made up of managers who reported to me.

I looked at small public corporations for an answer. They always have a board of directors. Some are inside directors, which mean they are part of management. There were outside directors as well who needed, by law, to be shareholders, but were not employees.

It was a bit different in our organization but all of our financial advisors were self-employed and were not "accountable" to me in the normal employer, employee sense.

I decided to form a board of four advisors who represented different years of experience and methods of operating. My initial plan was to meet quarterly, as public corporation boards do, to go over results etc.

This rarely happened but something else did. They became my sounding board. Whenever I was struggling with a situation or had an idea I was not sure about, we would get together and talk. Again, it was a 'safe' place so free speech was in place.

On one occasion I had a major concern. I thought about it a lot, knew something had to be done, came up with a workable

RESERVED FOR YOUR THOUGHTS

solution and called the board together. I went over everything with them, including my proposed solution. Then the shock came.

To a person, they said they did not think the issue was a concern at all and did not feel that anything had to be done. After I got off of the floor, I came to realize that they were right. Time showed that they were right.

If as a leader, we do not have access to outside thoughts, we can be guilty of making a decision that did not take the bigger picture into consideration. The more we think about *our* ideas, the more we are convinced that we are right.

Advisory groups like this can be set up in a dental office, sales or service organization, sport organization, golf club etc.

The other benefit of an advisory group is that they tend to take ownership in the whole organization which is very healthy.

A BOARD OF DIRECTORS or ADVISORY GROUP is easy to set up and if the meetings are truly a "safe" place, the value to the leader is immeasurable.

LESSON SIX
DEALING WITH CHANGE

Change is with us, always. Some changes are immediately seen as a positive, but not all of them.

When change happens, whether positive or negative, our LEADERSHIP skills are put to the test. Our associates will look to us for guidance and stability.

A leader must look at the situation from everyone's perspective, not just their own. Some changes can be averted, or altered in some way, but others must be accepted and dealt with. The attitude of the leader at this time will set the tone for how his associates respond.

GET vs. GOT

Only one letter is different in these two words but the message each delivers, is dramatically different.

GOT infers that you have no choice. "I don't like it. I don't know why THEY are doing this. Who do THEY think they are," etc.

GET says that "I am being given an opportunity".

Think about it. There is a major attitude difference here.

If a leader takes the "GOT" response, he emits a negative attitude and his associates will join the *why are they doing this to us* party. This starts a downhill spiral that is difficult to stop. At this point there is NO leadership happening. There is nothing but

RESERVED FOR YOUR THOUGHTS

confusion and frustration, and no guidance.

The GET leader will examine all options available, figure out how the change can be turned into a positive, and share his feelings with his people. When people can see what they have to do, realize that they will receive the assistance that they need to do it, stability returns to their lives.

ACCEPTING THE FACT THAT CHANGE WILL ALWAYS BE WITH US, how can a leader prepare, in advance, for "GET" opportunities that will undoubtedly come our way?

That's a tough one. Let's go to the next lesson for some ideas.

RESERVED FOR YOUR THOUGHTS

LESSON SEVEN
LIFE LONG LEARNING

A LEADER MUST STAY AHEAD OF THE CURVE.

A term to think about is LIFE LONG LEARNING.

When you stop growing, you die. Sounds dramatic, but is true.

If you are running a business, or a hospital, or a dental practice, products and/ or techniques are always improving. To be a leader you must know where each of these is going in the future.

Many professions require their members to take continuing education to keep their licence or professional status. Some people look at this requirement as a "make work project". Progressive leaders see this as an opportunity to grow. The **"GET" manager** thrives on personal and professional growth.

Reading new published articles that affect your career are a must. This should be part of your regular routine. Taking courses cost money and take valuable time, but should be in your annual time and financial budget.

Study clubs often provide you with new ideas and can be a place to safely test these ideas on a group of 'outsiders'.

Sometimes the changes that are coming are outside of your "comfort zone". Let's use technology as an example.

Some leaders are more of the inspirational, then the technical bent. How does that leader stay ahead of the curve?

HIRING PEOPLE BETTER THEN YOURSELF

We have all heard speakers say that they hire people better then themselves. I think we all know that often it is not the full truth.

Many "leaders" are intimidated by people who "know" more than they do.

A great leader knows his own strengths and hires people who can handle areas he is not comfortable with.

Many years ago, as Henry Ford was getting older, some directors of the Ford Motor Company tried to prove that he was incompetent and unable to lead the company. They actually took him to court to have him removed. To test his knowledge they asked him questions. Often his answer was that he did not know. Those directors thought they were winning their case. Finally Henry Ford said that although he did not know the answers he had buttons on his desk and when he needed an answer he pushed the appropriate button and an expert at the other end of the line could provide it. Henry Ford remained in charge.

If, as an example, technology is not your strength, hire the BEST people available and provide them with the best training and equipment.

This does not only apply to technology but to every other aspect of your business or career.

GREAT LEADERS stay ahead of the curve by committing themselves to LIFE LONG LEARNING and hiring top people who are better than they are in certain areas.

RESERVED FOR YOUR THOUGHTS

Utilizing the services of experts in required areas provide growth opportunities to your associates and stability in their lives.

RESERVED FOR YOUR THOUGHTS

LESSON EIGHT
AN IDEA PERSON

A LEADER IS AN *IDEA PERSON.*

Where do great ideas come from?

Reading, taking courses, visiting with our peers and associates, fills our mind with many thoughts and ideas. Unfortunately, we often get caught up in the day to day issues of our lives and those ideas remain dormant. One person told me that he didn't need to take any more courses because he already knew more than he was putting into practise. That is probably true for most of us.

When I was working I had about a 30 minute drive to the office. I found that when I turned the radio off it was a great time to think. I would often take one idea, or concern, and just think about it. Most times I would arrive at the office before any great "gems" flowed from my mind. But, every once in a while a "light bulb moment" would happen, and the things going through my mind would gel.

Sometimes we need "*patience to ponder*" before taking action.

Depending on what it was, I might call my board of directors together and tell them what I was thinking about. If it had merit we would start the process of implementing it. This is not rocket science. It requires no special training or skills. **Our mind is the most powerful computer ever created,** and the data in it, is never lost, but recall requires time, sometimes, "quiet" time.

We all have time to think, if we look for it. Driving our car, riding our bike, walking on the treadmill etc., can be "our" time, just to think.

An Excellent LEADER takes time to think.

RESERVED FOR YOUR THOUGHTS

INSPIRED LEADERS OF OUR TIME

President Kennedy said that before the end of the decade the United States would put a man on the moon. He had no idea how to fly or build a space ship. He set the stage and even though he never lived to see it achieved, it was.

Martin Luther King said, "I have a dream". He said this at a time, when in the south, there were *white only* water fountains and black people rode at the back of the bus. They were not even given the right to vote until the passing of the Civil Rights Act of 1964. In 2008 the U.S.A elected a black President. His dream never died.

Winston Churchill said, "We will never surrender". He inspired a nation that became used to hearing air raid sirens every night, through his oratory.

Chuck Noll, coach of the NFL Pittsburgh Steelers went 4-0 in Super Bowl games. The most Super Bowl wins by a coach, ever. Vince Lombardi went 9-1 in playoff games with the Green Bay Packers and the Super Bowl is named after him. Each of these great leaders had players on their teams that could do "their job" better than they could.

Nelson Mandela provided inspiration to a country while spending 30 years in prison. He never, ever, gave up. Neither did his followers.

RESERVED FOR YOUR THOUGHTS

WHAT HAVE WE LEARNED?

After reading the letters and notes given to me at the time of my retirement I tried to sum up what people wanted from an **INSPIRED LEADER**.

I narrowed it down to this:

1. "I CAN"
   A leader must whole heartedly believe, "We can do it." You can't fake it. Does that mean that a leader has no doubts? Of course not. This is not a dream world we live in. It means that leaders believe it can, and will get done and are prepared to do whatever it takes to make it happen. The people associated with him, believe him, and "buy in".

2. It isn't so much what a leader says, or what he does, but rather, WHO HE OR SHE IS.

   The problem is that most great leaders are anything but, perfect people. They often have many faults and weaknesses. I believe that what they have in common is that they provide a sense of STABILITY, and FOCUS. They are the core of the organization or team. Their basic standards are consistent, not wavering with every wind that comes along, and they can be counted on when the chips are down. They are fair.

This is not a "skill set", or a "trick" that can be learned.

It is **WHO YOU ARE**.

The key to becoming an INSPIRED LEADER is to have basic fundamental principles that stand the test of time.

So... Now What??

RESERVED FOR YOUR THOUGHTS

STEPS YOU CAN TAKE TO
BECOME AN INSPIRED LEADER

Read this book a few times, and think about how each of the ideas can apply to you and your specific environment. Focus on each lesson for one week.

1. Week one: Look for ways to show your appreciation of your people and **say THANKS**. At the end of the week I am confident you will have created a more positive work environment.

2. Week two: Think about your associates as **PEOPLE WITH LIVES**, and not just employees. Give them a chance to see you as a **PERSON WITH A LIFE** and not just their leader. Do this consciously for a week and then take some time to reflect and analyze how you feel about that experience.

3. Week three: Focus on **LISTENING** to your associates, **REALLY LISTENING**. You may discover that you were not as good a listener as you thought you were.

4. Week four: Keep doing what you have been doing during the previous three weeks, and then look at the rest of the lessons to see which of them you should start to implement.

There is an old adage that says "IT IS MORE BLESSED TO GIVE THAN RECEIVE".

GIVING of your thought, time and gratitude to the people you are associated with, will INSPIRE you as much as it will those, you give it to.

RESERVED FOR YOUR THOUGHTS

Congratulations!

YOU ARE ON YOUR WAY TO CREATING YOUR OWN LEGACY OF REMARKABLE LEADERSHIP!

ABOUT THE AUTHOR

Grant Norlin spent 31 years in Sales and Management with Sun Life Assurance Company of Canada.

He earned his Chartered Life Underwriter, Chartered Financial Consultant and Certified Financial Planner designations.

He was a member of the Million Dollar Round Table

While with Sun Life he received numerous awards and during his last year in management, won the coveted Presidents Cup as the top agency in Canada.

He was an active public speaker, addressing dozens of organizations in all parts of Canada and some areas in the USA.

Grant is past president of the Calgary and Edmonton Alberta, Life Insurance Managers Associations and served as the National President.

He was President of the Edmonton Life Underwriters Association and the Calgary Estate Planning Council.

He has served on numerous boards and committees including The Alberta Lung Association, Glencoe Golf and Country Club, two private oil companies plus residential community organizations.

Grant is married To Val. They have 4 married children and 10 terrific grandchildren.

Grant may be contacted at:

signatureofaleader@gmail.com

Made in the USA
San Bernardino, CA
17 February 2014